SPEECH

OF

WILLIAM H. SEWARD,

FOR THE

IMMEDIATE ADMISSION OF KANSAS INTO THE UNION.

SENATE OF THE UNITED STATES, APRIL 9, 1856.

Mr. PRESIDENT: To obtain empire is easy and common; to govern it well is difficult and rare indeed. I salute the Congress ot the United States in the exercise of its most important function, that of extending the Federal Constitution over added domains, and I salute especially the Senate in the most august of all its manifold characters, itself a Congress of thirty-one free, equal, sovereign States, assembled to decide whether the majestic and fraternal circle shall be opened to receive yet another free, equal, and sovereign State.

The Constitution prescribes only two qualifications for new States, namely—a substantial civil community, and a republican Government. Kansas has both of these.

The circumstances of Kansas, and her relations towards the Union, are peculiar, anomalous, and deeply interesting. The United States acquired the province of Louisiana, (which included the present Territory of Kansas,) from France, in 1803, by a treaty, in which they agreed that its inhabitants should be incorporated into the Federal Union, and admitted as soon as possible, according to the principles of the Constitution, to the enjoyment of all the rights, advantages, and immunities, of citizens of the United States. Nevertheless, Kansas was in 1820 assigned as a home for an indefinite period to several savage Indian tribes, and closed against immigration and all other than aboriginal civilization, but not without a contemporaneous pledge to the American people and to mankind, that neither Slavery nor involuntary servitude should be tolerated therein forever. In 1854, Congress directed a removal of the Indian tribes, and organized and opened Kansas to civilization, but by the same act rescinded the pledge of perpetual dedication to Freedom, and substituted for it another, which declared that the [future] people of Kansas should be left perfectly free to establish or to exclude Slavery, as they should decide through the action of a republican Government which Congress modeled and authorized them to establish, under the protection of the United States. Notwithstanding this latter pledge, when the newly associated people of Kansas, in 1855, were proceeding with the machinery of popular elections, in the manner prescribed by Congress, to choose legislative bodies for the purpose of organizing that republican Government, armed bands of invaders from the State of Missouri entered the Territory, seized the polls, overpowered or drove away the inhabitants, usurped the elective franchise, deposited false and spurious ballots without regard to regularity of qualification or of numbers, procured official certificates of the result by fraud and force, and thus created and constituted legislative bodies to act for and in the name of the people of the Territory. These legislative bodies afterward assembled, assumed to be a legitimate Legislature, set forth a code of municipal laws, created public offices and filled them with officers appointed for considerable periods by themselves, and thus established a complete and effective foreign tyranny over the people of the Territory. These high-handed transactions were consummated with the expressed purpose of establishing African Slavery as a permanent institution within the Territory by force, in violation of the natural rights of the people solemnly guaranteed to them by the Congress of the United States. The President of the United States has been an accessory to these political transactions, with full complicity in regard to the purpose for which they were committed. He has adopted the usurpation, and made it his own, and he is now maintaining it with the military arm of the Republic. Thus Kansas has been revolutionized, and she now lies subjugated and prostrate at the foot of the President of the United States, while he, through the agency of a foreign tyranny established within her borders, is forcibly introducing and establishing Slavery there, in contempt and defiance of the organic law. These extraordinary transactions have been attended by civil commotions, in which property, life, and liberty, have been exposed to violence, and these commotions still continue to threaten not only the Territory itself, but also the adjacent States, with the calamities and disasters of civil war.

I am fully aware of the gravity of the charges against the President of the United States which this statement of the condition and relations of Kansas imports. I shall proceed, without fear and without reserve, to make them good. The maxim, that a sacred veil must be drawn over the beginning of all Governments, does not hold under our system. I shall first call the accuser into the presence of the Senate—then examine the defences which the President has made—and, last, submit the evidences by which he is convicted.

The people of Kansas know whether these charges are true or false. They have adopted them, and, on the ground of the high political necessity which the wrongs they have endured, and are yet enduring, and the dangers through which they have already passed, and the perils to which they are yet exposed, have created, they have provisionally organized themselves as a State, and that State is now here, by its two chosen Senators and one Representative, standing outside at the doors of Congress, applying to be admitted into the Union, as a means of relief indispensable for the purposes of peace, freedom, and safety. This new State is the President's responsible accuser.

The President of the United States, without waiting for the appearance of his accuser at the capital, anticipated the accusations, and submitted his defences against them to Congress. The first one of these defences was contained in his annual message, which was communicated to Congress on the 30th of December, 1855. I examine it. You shall see at once that the President's mind was oppressed—was full of something, too large and burdensome to be concealed, and yet too critical to be told.

Mark, if you please, the state of the case at that time. So early as August, 1855, the people of Kansas had denounced the Legislature. They had at voluntary elections chosen Mr. A. H. Reeder to represent them in the present Congress, instead of J. W. Whitfield, who held a certificate of election under the authority of the Legislature. They had also, on the 23d day of October, 1855, by similar voluntary elections, constituted at Topeka an organic Convention, which framed a Constitution for the projected State. They had also, on the 15th of December, 1855, at similar voluntary elections, adopted that Constitution, and its tenor was fully known. It provided for elections to be held throughout the new State on the 15th of January, 1856, to fill the offices created by it, and it also required the Executive and Legislative officers, thus to be chosen, to assemble at Topeka on the 4th day of March, 1856, to inaugurate the new State provisionally, and to take the necessary means for the appointment of Senators, who, together with a Representative already chosen, should submit the Constitution to Congress at an early day, and apply for the admission of the State of Kansas into the Union. All these proceedings had been based on the grounds that the Territorial authorities of Kansas had been established by armed foreign usurpation, and were nevertheless sustained by the President of the United States. A constitutional obligation required the President "to give to Congress," in his annual message, "information of the state of the Union." Here is all "the information" which the President gave to Congress concerning the events in Kansas, and its relations to the Union:

"In the Territory of Kansas there have been 'acts prejudicial to good order, but as yet none 'have occurred under circumstances to justify 'the interposition of the Federal Executive. 'That could only be in case of obstruction to 'Federal law, or of organized resistance to Territorial law, assuming the character of insurrection, which, if it should occur, it would be my 'duty promptly to overcome and suppress. I 'cherish the hope, however, that the occurrence 'of any such untoward event will be prevented 'by the sound sense of the people of the Territory, who, by its organic law, possessing the 'right to determine their own domestic institutions, are entitled, while deporting themselves 'peacefully, to the free exercise of that right, and 'must be protected in the enjoyment of it, without interference on the part of the citizens of 'any of the States."

This information implies, that no invasion, usurpation, or tyranny, has been committed within the Territory by strangers; and that the provisional State organization now going forward is not only unnecessary, but also prejudicial to good order, and insurrectionary. It menaces the people of Kansas with a threat, that the President will "overcome and suppress" them. It mocks them with a promise, that, if they shall hereafter deport themselves properly, under the control of authorities by which they have been disfranchised, in determining institutions which have been already forcibly determined for them by foreign invasion, that then they "must be protected against interference by citizens of any of the States."

The President, however, not content with a statement so obscure and unfair, devotes a third part of the annual message to argumentative speculations bearing on the character of his accuser. Each State has two and no more Senators in the Senate of the United States. In determining the apportionment of Representatives in the House of Representatives, and in the electoral colleges among the States, three-fifths of all the slaves in any State are enumerated. The slaveholding or non-slaveholding character of a State is determined, not at the time of its admission into the Union as a State, but at that earlier period of its political life in which, being called a Territory, it is politically dependent on the United States, or on some foreign sovereign. Slavery is tolerated in some of the States, and forbidden in others. Affecting the industrial and economical systems of the several States, as Slavery and Freedom do, this diversity of practice concerning them early worked out a corresponding difference of conditions, interests, and ambitions, among the States, and divided and arrayed them into two classes. The balance of political power between these two classes in the Federal system is sensibly affected by the accession of any new State to either of them. Each State therefore watches jealously the settlement, growth, and inchoate slaveholding and non-slaveholding characters of Territories, which may ultimately come into the Union as States. It has resulted from these circumstances, that Slavery, in relations purely political and absolutely Federal, is an element which enters with more or less activity into many national questions of finance, of revenue, of expenditure, of protection, of free trade, of patronage, of peace, of war, of annexation, of defence, and of conquest, and modifies opinions concerning constructions of the Constitution, and the distribution of powers between the Union and the several States by which it is constituted. Slavery, under these political and Federal aspects alone, enters into the transactions in Kansas, with which the President and Congress are concerned. Nevertheless, he disingenuously alludes to those transactions in his defence, as if they were identified with that moral discussion of Slavery which he regards as odious and alarming, and without any other claim to consideration. Thus he alludes to the question before us as belonging to a "political agitation" "concerning a matter which consists to a great extent of exaggeration of inevitable evils, or over-zeal in social improvement, or mere imagination of grievance, having but a remote connection with any of the constitutional functions of the Federal Government, and menacing the stability of the Constitution and the integrity of the Union."

In like manner the President assails and stigmatizes those who defend and maintain the cause of Kansas, as "men of narrow views and sectional purposes," "engaged in those wild and chimerical schemes of social change which are generated one after another in the unstable minds of visionary sophists and interested agitators"—"mad men, raising the storm of frenzy and faction," "sectional agitators," "enemies of the Constitution, who have surrendered themselves so far to a fanatical devotion to the supposed interests of the relatively few Africans in the United States, as totally to abandon and disregard the interests of the twenty-five millions of Americans, and trample under foot the injunctions of moral and constitutional obligation, and to engage in plans of vindictive hostility against those who are associated with them in the enjoyment of the common heritage of our free institutions." Sir, the President's defence on this occasion, if not a matter simply personal, is at least one of temporary and ephemeral importance. Possibly, all the advantages he will gain by transferring to his accuser a portion of the popular prejudice against Abolition and Abolitionists, can be spared to him. It would be wise, however, for those whose interests are inseparable from Slavery, to reflect that Abolition will gain an equivalent benefit from the identification of the President's defence with their cherished institution. Abolition is a slow but irrepressible uprising of principles of natural justice and humanity, obnoxious to prejudice, because they conflict inconveniently with existing material, social, and political interests. It belongs to others than statesmen, charged with the care of present interests, to conduct the social reformation of mankind in its broadest bearings. I leave to Abolitionists their own work of self-vindication. I may, however, remind slaveholders that there is a time when oppression and persecution cease to be effectual against such movements; and then the odium they have before unjustly incurred becomes an element of strength and power. Christianity, blindly maligned during three centuries, by Prætors, Governors, Senates, Councils, and Emperors, towered above its enemies in a fourth; and even the cross on which its Founder had expired, and which therefore was the emblem of its shame, became the sign under which it went forth evermore thereafter, conquering and to conquer. Abolition is yet only in its first century.

The President raises in his defence a false issue, and elaborates an irrelevant argument to prove that Congress has no right or power, nor has any sister State any right or power, to interfere within a slave State, by legislation or force, to abolish Slavery therein—as if you, or I, or any other responsible man, ever maintained the contrary.

The President distorts the Constitution from its simple text, so as to make it expressly and directly defend, protect, and guaranty African Slavery. Thus he alleges that "the Government" which resulted from the Revolution was a "Federal Republic of the free white men of the Colonies," whereas, on the contrary, the Declaration of Independence asserts the political equality of all men, and even the Constitution itself carefully avoids any political recognition not merely of Slavery, but of the diversity of races. The President represents the Fathers as having contemplated and provided for a permanent increase of the number of slaves in some of the States, and therefore forbidden Congress to touch Slavery in the way of attack or offence, and as having therefore also placed it under the general safeguard of the Constitution; whereas the Fathers, by authorizing Congress to abolish the African slave trade after 1808, as a means of attack, inflicted on Slavery in the States a blow, of which they expected it to languish immediately, and ultimately to expire.

The President closes his defence in the annual message with a deliberate assault, very incongruous in such a place, upon some of the Northern States. At the same time he abstains, with marked caution, from naming the accused States. They, however, receive a compliment at his hands, by way of giving keenness to his rebuke, which enables us to identify them. They are Northern States "which were conspicuous in founding the Republic." All of the original Northern States were conspicuous in that great transaction. All of them, therefore, are accused. The offence charged is, that they disregard their constitutional obligations, and although "conscious of their inability to heal admitted and palpable social evils of their own confessedly within their jurisdiction, they engage in an offensive, hope-

'less, and illegal undertaking, to reform the do-'mestic institutions of the Southern States, at the 'peril of the very existence of the Constitution, 'and of all the countless benefits which it has 'conferred." I challenge the President to the proof, in behalf of Massachusetts; although I have only the interest common to all Americans and to all men in her great fame. What one corporate or social evil is there, of which she is conscious, and conscious also of inability to heal it? Is it ignorance, prejudice, bigotry, vice, crime, public disorder, poverty, or disease, afflicting the minds or the bodies of her people? There she stands. Survey her universities, colleges, academies, observatories, primary schools, Sunday schools, penal codes, and penitentiaries. Descend into her quarries, walk over her fields and through her gardens, observe her manufactories of a thousand various fabrics, watch her steamers ascending every river and inlet on your own coast, and her ships displaying their canvass on every sea; follow her fishermen in their adventurous voyages from her own and adjacent bays to the icy ocean under either pole; and then return and enter her hospitals, which cure or relieve suffering humanity in every condition and at every period of life, from the lying-in to the second childhood, and which not only restore sight to the blind, and hearing to the deaf, and speech to the dumb, but also bring back wandering reason to the insane, and teach even the idiot to think! Massachusetts, sir, is a model of States, worthy of all honor; and though she was most conspicuous of all the States in the establishment of republican institutions here, she is even more conspicuous still for the municipal wisdom with which she has made them contribute to the welfare of her people, and to the greatness of the Republic itself.

In behalf of New York, for whom it is my right and duty to speak, I defy the Presidential accuser. Mark her tranquil magnanimity, which becomes a State for whose delivery from tyranny Schuyler devised and labored, who received her political Constitution from Hamilton, her intellectual and physical development from Clinton, and her lessons in humanity from Jay. As she waves her wand over the continent, trade forsakes the broad natural channels which conveyed it before to the Delaware and Chesapeake bays and to the Gulfs of St. Lawrence and Mexico, and obedient to her command pours itself through her artificial channels into her own once obscure seaport. She stretches her wand again towards the ocean, and the commerce of all the continents concentrates itself at her feet; and with it, strong and full floods of immigration ride in, contributing labor, capital, art, valor, and enterprise, to perfect and embellish our ever-widening empire.

When, and on what occasion, has Massachusetts or New York officiously and illegally intruded herself within the jurisdiction of sister States, to modify or reform their institutions? No, no, sir. Their faults have been quite different. They have conceded too often and too much for their own just dignity and influence in Federal Administration, to the querulous complaints of the States in whose behalf the President arraigns them. I thank the President for the insult which, though so deeply unjust, was perhaps needful to arouse them to their duty in this great emergency.

The President, in this connection, reviews the acquisitions of new domain, the organization of new Territories, and the admission of new States, and arrives at results which must be as agreeably surprising to the slave States, as they are astounding to the free States. He finds that the former have been altogether guiltless of political ambition, while he convicts the latter not only of unjust territorial aggrandizement, but also of false and fraudulent clamor against the slave States, to cover their own aggressions. Notwithstanding the President's elaborated misconceptions, these historical facts remain, namely—that no acquisition whatever has ever been made at the instance of the free States, and with a view to their aggrandizement: that Louisiana and Florida, incidentally acquired for general and important national objects, have already yielded to the slave States three States of their own class, while Texas was avowedly annexed as a means of security to Slavery, and one slave State has been already admitted from that acquisition, and Congress has stipulated for the admission of four more: that by way of equivalent for the admission of California a free State, the slave States have obtained a virtual repeal of the Mexican law which forbade Slavery in New Mexico and Utah; and that, as a consequence of that extraordinary legislation, Congress has also rescinded the prohibition of Slavery, which, in 1820, was extended over all of that part of Louisiana, except Missouri, which lies north of 36° 30′ of north latitude. Sir, the real crime of the Northern States is this: they are forty degrees too high on the arc of north latitude.

I dismiss for the present the President's first defence against the accusation of the new State of Kansas.

On the 24th of January, 1856, when no important event had happened which was unknown at the date of the President's annual message, he submitted to Congress his second defence, in the form of a special message. In this paper, the President deplores, as the cause of all the troubles which have occurred in Kansas, delays of the organization of the Territory, which have been permitted by the Governor, Mr. Reeder. The organic law was passed by Congress on the 31st of May, 1854, but on that day there was not one lawful elector, citizen, or inhabitant, within the Territory, while the question, whether Slavery or universal Freedom should be established there, was devolved practically on the first Legislative bodies to be elected by the people who were to become thereafter the inhabitants of Kansas. The election for the first Legislative bodies was appointed by the Governor to be held on the 30th of March, 1855; and the 2d day of July, 1855, was designated for the organization of the Legislative Assembly. The only civilized community that was in contact with the new Territory was Missouri, a slaveholding State, at whose instance the prohibition of Slavery within the Territory had been abrogated, so that she might attempt to colonize it with slaves. Immigrants were invited not only from all parts of the United States, but also from all other parts of the world, with a pledge that the people of the new Territory should be left perfectly free to establish or prohibit Slavery. A special election, however, was held within the Territory on the 29th day of November, 1854, without any preliminary census of the inhabitants, for the purpose of choosing a Delegate who might sit without a right to vote in Congress, during the second session of the Thirty-third Congress, which was to begin on the first Monday of December, 1854, and to end on the third day of March, 1855. Mr. J. W. Whitfield was certified to be elected. There were vehement complaints of illegality in the election, but his title was nevertheless not contested, for the palpable reasons, that an investigation under the circumstances of the Territory, during so short a session of Congress, would be impossible, and that the question was of inconsiderable magnitude. Yet the President laments that the Governor neglected to order the first election for the Legislative bodies of the new Territory to be held simultaneously with that hurried Congressional election. He assigns his reasons: "Any question 'appertaining to the qualifications of persons 'voting as the people of the Territory would (in 'that case, incidentally) have necessarily passed 'under the supervision of Congress, (meaning the 'House of Representatives,) and would have been 'determined before conflicting passions had been 'inflamed by time, and before an opportunity 'would have been afforded for systematic interfer-'ence by the people of individual States." Could the President, in any explicit arrangement of words, more distinctly have confessed his disappointment in failing to secure a merely formal election of Legislative bodies within the Territory, in fraud of the organic law, of the people of Kansas, and of the cause of natural justice and humanity?

The President then proceeds to launch severe denunciations against what he calls a propagandist attempt to colonize the Territory with opponents of Slavery. The whole American Continent has been undergoing a process of colonization, in many forms, throughout a period of three hundred and fifty years. The only common element of all those forms was propagandism. Were not the voyages of Columbus progagandist expeditions, under the auspices of the Pope of Rome? Was not the wide occupation of Spanish America a propagandism of the Catholic Church? The settlement of Massachusetts by the Pilgrims; of the New Netherlands by the Reformers of Holland; the later plantation of the Mohawk valley by the Palatines; the establishment of Pennsylvania by the Friends; the mission of the Moravians at Bethlehem, in the same State; the foundation of Maryland by Lord Baltimore and his colony of British Catholics; the settlement of Jamestown by the Cavaliers and Churchmen of England; that of South Carolina by the Huguenots: Were not all these propagandist colonizations? Was not Texas settled by a colony of slaveholders, and California by companies of freemen? Yet never before did any Prince, King, Emperor, or President, denounce such colonizations. Does any law of nature or nations forbid them? Does any public authority quarantine, on the ground of opinion, the ships which are continually pouring into the gates of New York whole religious societies from Ireland, Wales, Germany, and Norway, with their pastors, and clerks, and choirs?

But the President charges that the propagandists entered Kansas with a design to "anticipate 'and force the determination of the Slavery 'question within the Territory," (in favor of Freedom,) forgetting, nevertheless, that he has only just before deplored a failure of his own to anticipate and force the determination of that question in favor of Slavery, by a *coup-de-main*, in advance even of their departure from their homes in the Atlantic States and in Europe. He charges, moreover, that the propagandists designed to "prevent the free and natural action of the in-'habitants in the intended organization of the 'Territory," when, in fact, they were pursuing the only free and natural course to organize it by immigrating and becoming permanent inhabitants, citizens, and electors, of Kansas. Not one unlawful or turbulent act has been hitherto charged against any one of the propagandists of Freedom. Mark, now, an extraordinary inconsistency of the President. On the 29th of June, 1854, only twenty-nine days after the opening of the Territory, and before one of these emigrants had reached Kansas, or even Missouri, a propagandist association, but not of emigrants, named the Platte County Self-Defensive Association, assembled at Weston, on the western border of Missouri, in the interest of Slavery; and it published, through the organ of the President of the United States at that place, a resolution, that "when 'called upon by any citizen of Kansas, its mem-'bers would hold themselves in readiness to 'assist in removing any and all emigrants who 'should go there under the aid of Northern Emi-'grant Societies." This association afterward often made good its atrocious threats, by violence against the property, peace, and lives, of unoffending citizens of Kansas. But the President of the United States, so far from denouncing it, does not even note its existence.

The majority of the Committee on Territories ingeniously elaborate the President's charge, and arraign Massachusetts, her Emigrant Aid Society, and her emigrants. What has Massachusetts done, worthy of censure? Before the Kansas organic law was passed by Congress, Massachusetts, on application, granted to some of her citizens, who were engaged in "taking up" new lands in Western regions, one of those common charters which are used by all associations, industrial, moral, social, scientific, and religious, now-a-days, instead of copartnerships, for the more convenient transaction of their fiscal affairs. The actual capital is some $60,000. Neither the granting of the charter, nor any legislative action of the association under it, was morally wrong. To emigrate from one State or Territory singly, or in company with others, with or without incorporation by statute, is a right of every citizen of the United States, as it is a right of every freeman in the world. The State that denies this right is a tyranny—the subject to whom it is denied is a slave. Such free emigration is the chief element of American progress and civilization. Without it, there could be no community, no political Territory, no State in Kansas. Without it, there could have been no United States of America. To retain and carry into Kansas cherished political as well as moral, social, and religious convictions, is a right of every emigrant. Must emigrants to that Territory carry there only their persons, and leave behind their minds and souls, disembodied and wandering in their native lands? They only are fit founders of a State who exercise independence of opinion; and it is to the exercise of that right that our new States, equally with all the older ones, owe their intelligence and vigor.

"There are, who, distant from their native soil,
Still for their own and country's glory toil;
While some, fast rooted to their parent spot,
In life are useless, and in death, forgot."

It is not morally wrong for Massachusetts to aid her sons, by a charter, to do what in itself is innocent and commendable. The President and the majority of the committee maintain that such associations are in violation of national or at least of international laws. Here is the Constitution of the United States, and here are the Statutes at Large, in ten volumes octavo. Let the President or his defenders point out the inhibition. They specify, particularly, that the action of the State violates a law of comity, which regulates the intercourse of independent States, and especially the intercourse between the members of the Federal Union. Here are Vattel and Burlamaqui. Let them point out in these pages this law of comity. There is no law of comity which forbids nations from permitting and encouraging emigration, on the ground of opinion. Moreover, Slavery is an outlaw under the law of nations. Still further, the Constitution of the United States has expressly incorporated into itself all of the laws of comity, for regulating the intercourse between independent States, which it deems proper to adopt. Whatever is forbidden expressly by the Constitution is unlawful. Whatever is not forbidden is lawful. The supposed law of comity is not incorporated into the Constitution.

With the aid of the Committee on Territories, we discover that the emigrants from Massachusetts have violated the supposed national laws, not by any unlawful conduct of their own, but by provoking the unlawful and flagitious conduct of the invaders of Kansas. "They passed through Missouri 'in large numbers, using violent language, and 'giving unmistakable indications of their hostility 'to the domestic institutions of that State," and thus "they created apprehensions that the object 'of the Emigrant Aid Company was to *abolitionize* 'Kansas, as a means of prosecuting a relentless 'warfare upon the institution of Slavery within 'the limits of Missouri, which apprehensions, increasing with the progress of events, ultimately 'became settled convictions of the people of 'western Missouri."

Missouri builds railroads, steamboats, and wharves. It cannot be, therefore, that the mere "largeness of the numbers" of the Eastern travellers offended or alarmed the borderers. I confess my surprise that the sojourners used violent language. It seems unlike them. I confess my greater surprise that the borderers were disturbed so deeply by mere words. It seems unlike them. Which of the domestic institutions of Missouri were those against which the travellers manifested determined hostility? Not certainly her manufactories, banks, railroads, churches, and schools. All these are domestic institutions held in high respect by the men of Massachusetts, and are just such ones as these emigrants are now establishing in Kansas. It was therefore African Slavery alone, a peculiar domestic institution of Missouri, against which their hostility was directed. Waiving a suspicious want of proof of the unwise conduct charged against them, I submit that clearly they did not thereby endanger that peculiar institution in Missouri, for they passed directly through that State into Kansas. How, then, were the borderers provoked? The Missourians inferred, from the language and demeanor of the travellers, that they would *abolitionize* Kansas, and thereafter, by means of Kansas abolitionized, prosecute a relentless warfare against Slavery in Missouri. Far-seeing statesmen are these Missouri borderers, but less deliberate than far-sighted. Kansas was not to be abolitionized. It had never been otherwise than abolitionized. Abolitionized Kansas would constitute no means for the prosecution of such a warfare. Missouri lies adjacent to abolitionized Iowa on the north, and to abolitionized Illinois on the east, yet neither of those States has ever been used for such designs. How could this fearful enemy prosecute a warfare against Slavery in Missouri? Only by buying the plantations of her citizens at their own prices, and so qualifying themselves to speak their hostility through the ballot-boxes? Could apprehensions so absurd justify the invasion of Kansas? Are the people of Kansas to be disfranchised and trodden down by the President of the United States, in punishment for any extravagance of emigrants, in Missouri, on the way to that Territory?

Such is the President's second defence, so far as it presents new matter in avoidance of the accusation of the new State of Kansas.

I proceed, in the third place, to establish the truth of the accusations. Of what sort must the proofs be? Manifestly only such as the circumstances of the case permit to exist. Not engrossed documents, authenticated by executive, judicial, or legislative officers. The transactions occurred in an unorganized country. All the authorities subsequently established in the Territory are implicated, all the complainants disfranchised. Only presumptive evidence, derived from the contemporaneous statements and actions of the parties concerned, can be required.

Such presumptive evidence is derived from the nature and character of the President's defences. Why did the President plead at all on the 31st of December last, when the new State of Kansas was yet unorganized, and could not appear here to prefer her accusations until the 23d of March? Why, if he must answer so prematurely, did he not plead a general and direct denial? If he must plead specially, why did he not set forth the facts, instead of withholding all actual information concerning the case? Why, since, instead of defending himself, he must implead his accuser, did he not state, at least, the ground on which that accuser claimed to justify the conduct of which he complained? Why did he threaten "to overcome and suppress" the people of Kansas, as insurrectionists, if he did not mean to terrify them, and to prevent their appearing here, or at least to prejudice their cause? Why did he mock them with a promise of protection thereafter, against interference by citizens of other States, if they should deport themselves peacefully and submissively to the Territorial authorities, if no cause for apprehending such interference had already been given by previous invasion? Why did he labor to embarrass his accuser by identifying her cause with the subject of abolition of Slavery, and stigmatize her supporters with opprobrious epithets, and impute to them depraved and seditious motives? Why did he interpose the false and impertinent issue, whether one State could intervene by its laws or by force to abolish Slavery in another State? Why did he distort the Constitution, and present it as expressly guarantying the perpetuity of Slavery? Why did he arraign so unnecessarily and so unjustly, not one, but all of the original Northern States? Why did he drag into this case, where only Kansas is concerned, a studied, partial, and prejudicial history of the past enlargements of the national domain, and of the past contests between the slave States and the free States, in their rivalry for the balance of power?

Why did not the President rest content with one such attack on the character and conduct of the new State of Kansas, in anticipating her coming, if he felt assured that she really had no merit on which to stand? Why did he submit a second plea in advance? Why in this plea does he deplore the delays which prevented the Missouri borderers from effecting the conquest of Kansas, and the establishment of Slavery therein, at the time of the Congressional election held in November, 1854, in fraud of the Kansas law, and of justice and humanity? Why, without reason, or authority of public or of national law, does he denounce Massachusetts, her Emigrant Aid Society, and her emigrants? If "propagandist" emigrations must be denounced, why does he spare the Platte County Self-Defensive Association? Why does he charge Governor Reeder with "failing to put forth all his energies to prevent or counteract the tendencies to illegality which are found to exist in all imperfectly organized and newly associated countries," if, indeed, no "illegality" has occurred there? While thus, by implication, admitting that such illegality has occurred in Kansas, why does he not tell us its nature and extent? Why, when Gov. Reeder was implicated in personal conduct, not criminal, but incongruous with his official relations, did the President retain him in office until after he had proclaimed at Easton that Kansas had been subjugated by the borderers of Missouri, and why, after he had done so, and had denounced the Legislature, did the President remove him for the same pre-existing cause only? Why does the President admit that the election for the legislative bodies of Kansas was held under circumstances inauspicious to a truthful and legal result, if, nevertheless, the result attained was indeed a truthful and legal one? On what evidence does the President ground his statement, that after that election, there were *mutual* complaints of usurpation, fraud, and violence, when we hear from no other quarter of such complaints made by the party that prevailed? If there were such mutual accusations, and even if they rested on probable grounds, would that fact abate the right of the people of Kansas to a Government of their own, securing a safe and well-ordered freedom? Why does the President argue that the Governor (Mr. Reeder) alone had the power to receive and consider the returns of the election of the Legislative bodies, and that he certified those returns in fifteen out of the twenty-two districts, when he knows that the Governor, being his own agent, gave the certificates, on the ground that the returns were technically correct, and that the illegality complained of was in the conduct of the elections, and in the making up of the returns by the judges, and that the terror of the armed invasion prevented all complaints of this kind from being presented to the Governor? Why does the President repose on the fact that the Governor, on the ground of informality in the returns, rejected the members who were chosen in the seven other districts, and ordered new elections therein, and certified in favor of the persons then chosen, when he knows that the majority, elected in the fifteen districts, expelled at once the persons chosen at such second elections, and admitted those originally returned as elected in these seven districts, on the ground that the Governor's rejection of them, and the second elections which he ordered, were unauthorized and illegal? Why does the President, although omitting to mention this last fact, nevertheless justify the expulsion of these newly elected members, on the ground that it was authorized by parliamentary law, when he knows that there was no parliamentary or other law existing in the Territory, but the organic act of Congress, which conferred no such power on the Legislature? Why was Governor Reeder replaced by Mr. Shannon, who immediately proclaimed that the Legislative bodies which his predecessor had denounced were the legitimate Legislature of the Territory? Why does the President plead that the subject of the alleged Missourian usurpation and tyranny in Kansas was one which, by its nature, appertained exclusively to the jurisdiction of the local authorities of the Territory, when, if the charges were true, there were no legitimate local authorities within the Territory? Is a foreign usurpation in a defenceless Territory of the United States to be tolerated, if only it be successful? And is the Government *de facto*, by whomsoever usurped, and with whatever tyranny exercised, entitled to demand obedience from the people, and to be recognised by the President of the United States? Why does he plead, that "whatever irregularities may have occurred, it is now too late to raise the question?" Is there nothing left but endurance to citizens of the United States, constituting a whole political community of men, women, and children—an incipient American State—subjugated and oppressed? Must they sit down in peace, abandoned, contented, and despised? Why does he plead, that "at least it is a question as to which, neither 'now, nor at any previous time, has the least 'possible legal authority been possessed by the 'President of the United States?" Did any magistrate ever before make such an exhibition of ambitious imbecility? Cannot Congress clothe him with power to act, and is it not his duty to ask power to remove usurpation and subvert tyranny in a Territory of the United States? Are these the tone, the tenor, and the staple, of a defence, where the accused is guiltless, and the crimes charged were never committed? The President virtually confesses all the transactions charged, by thus presenting a connected system of maxims and principles, invented to justify them.

I proceed, however, to clinch conviction by direct and positive proofs: First, the statements of the party which has been overborne. General Pomeroy and his associates, in behalf of the State of Kansas, make this representation concerning the Congressional election held in the Territory on the 30th of November, 1854:

"The first ballot-box that was opened upon 'our virgin soil was closed to us by overpowering numbers and impending force. So bold and 'reckless were our invaders, that they cared not 'to conceal their attack. They came upon us, 'not in the guise of voters, to steal away our 'franchise, but boldly and openly, to snatch it 'with a strong hand. They came directly from 'their own homes, and in compact and organized bands, with arms in hand and provisions for 'the expedition, marched to our polls, and, when 'their work was done, returned whence they came. 'It is unnecessary to enter into the details; it is 'enough to say that in three districts, in which, 'by the most irrefragable evidence, there were not 'one hundred and fifty voters, most of whom refused to participate in the mockery of the elective franchise, these invaders polled over a thousand votes."

In regard to the election of the 30th of March, 1855, the same party states:

"They (the Missourians) arrived at their several destinations the night before the election, 'and having pitched their camps and placed their 'sentries, waited for the coming day. Baggage 'wagons were there, with arms and ammunition 'enough for a protracted fight, and among them two 'brass field-pieces, ready charged. They came with 'drums beating and flags flying, and their leaders 'were of the most prominent and conspicuous 'men of their respective States. In the morning 'they surrounded the polls, armed with guns, 'bowie-knives, and revolvers, and declared their 'determination to vote at all hazards, and in 'spite of all consequences. If the judges could 'be made to subserve their purposes, and receive 'their votes, and if no obstacle was cast in their 'way, their leaders exerted themselves to preserve peace and order in the conduct of the 'election; but at the same time did not hesitate 'to declare, that if not allowed to vote, they 'would proceed to any extremity in destruction 'of property and life. If the control of the polls 'could not be had otherwise, the judges were by 'intimidation, and, if necessary, by violence, prevented from performing their duty, or, if unyielding in this respect, were driven from their 'post, and the vacancy filled in form by the persons on the ground; and whenever by any means 'they had obtained the control of the board, the 'foreign vote was promiscuously poured in, without discrimination or reserve, or the slightest 'care to conceal its nefarious illegality. At one 'of the polls, two of the judges having manfully stood up in the face of the armed mob, 'and declared they would do their duty, one portion of the mob commenced to tear down the 'house, another proceeded to break in the door 'of the judges' room, whilst others, with drawn 'knives, posted themselves at the window, with 'the proclaimed purpose of killing any voter who 'would allow himself to be sworn. Voters were 'dragged from the window, because they would 'not show their tickets, or vote at the dictation 'of the mob; and the invaders declared openly, 'at the polls, that they would cut the throats of 'the judges, if they did not receive their votes 'without requiring an oath as to their residence. 'The room was finally forced, and the judges, 'surrounded by an armed and excited crowd, 'were offered the alternative of resignation or 'death, and five minutes were allowed for their 'decision. The ballot-box was seized, and, amid 'shouts of 'Hurrah for Missouri,' was carried 'into the mob. The two menaced judges then 'left the ground, together with all the resident 'citizens, except a few who acted in the outrage, 'because the result expected from it corresponded 'to their own views.

"When an excess of the foreign force was found 'to be had at one poll, detachments were sent to 'the others. * * * * A minister of the 'Gospel, who refused to accede to the demands 'of a similar mob of some 400 armed and organized men, was driven by violence from his post, 'and the vacancy filled by themselves. * * * '* Another clergyman, for the expression of 'his opinion, was assaulted and beaten. * * ' * * The inhabitants of the district, powerless to resist the abundant supply of arms and 'ammunition, organized preparation, and overwhelming numbers of the foreigners, left the 'polls without voting. * * * In the Lawrence district, one voter was fired at, as he was 'driven from the election ground. * * * 'Finding they had a greater force than was necessary for that poll, some 200 men were drafted 'from the number, and sent off under the proper 'officers to another district, after which they still 'polled from this camp 700 votes. * * * In 'the 4th and 7th districts, the invaders came 'together in an armed and organized body, with 'trains of fifty wagons, besides horsemen, and, 'the night before election, pitched their camps 'in the vicinity of the polls, and having appointed their own judges, in place of those who, from 'intimidation or otherwise, failed to attend, they 'voted without any proof of residence. In these 'two election districts, where the census shows '100 voters, there were polled 314 votes, and last 'fall 765 votes, although a large part of the act- 'ual residents did not vote on either occasion. '* * * * From a careful examination of 'the returns, we are satisfied that over 3,000 'votes were thus cast by the citizens and resi- 'dents of the States."

I place in opposition to these statements of the party that was overborne, the statements of the party that prevailed, beginning with signals of the attack, and ending with celebrations of the victory.

General Stringfellow addressed the invaders in Missouri, on the eve of the election of March 30, 1855, thus:

"To those who have qualms of conscience as 'to violating laws, State or National, the time 'has come when such impositions must be dis- 'regarded, as your rights and property are in 'danger; and I advise you, one and all, to enter 'every election district in Kansas, in defiance of 'Reeder and his vile myrmidons, and vote, at the 'point of the bowie-knife and revolver. Neither 'give nor take quarter, as our case demands it. 'It is enough that the slaveholding interest wills 'it, from which there is no appeal. What right 'has Governor Reeder to rule Missourians in 'Kansas? His proclamation and prescribed 'oath must be repudiated. It is your interest 'to do so. Mind that Slavery is established 'where it is not prohibited."

The Kansas *Herald*, an organ of both the Administration and the Pro-Slavery party, announced the result of the Legislative election in the Territory immediately afterwards, as follows:

"Yesterday was a proud and glorious day for 'the friends of Southern Rights. The triumph of 'the Pro-Slavery party is complete and over- 'whelming. Come on, Southern men! Bring 'your slaves, and fill up the Territory! Kansas 'is saved!"

The *Squatter Sovereign*, published in Missouri, thus announced the result of the election, the day after it closed:

"INDEPENDENCE, *March* 31, 1855.

"Several hundred emigrants from Kansas have 'just entered our city. They were preceded by 'the Westport and Independence brass bands. 'They came in at the west side of the public 'square, and proceeded entirely around it, the 'bands cheering us with fine music, and the em- 'igrants with good news. Immediately following 'the bands were about two hundred horsemen 'in regular order; following these were one hun- 'dred and fifty wagons, carriages, &c. They 'gave repeated cheers for Kansas and Missouri. 'They report that not an Anti-Slavery man will 'be in the Legislature of Kansas. We have made 'a clean sweep."

A letter written at Brunswick, in Missouri, dated April 20th, 1855, and published in the New York *Herald*, a Pro-Slavery journal, says that "from five to seven thousand men started 'from Missouri to attend the election, some to 'remove, but the most to return to their families, 'with an intention, if they liked the Territory, to 'make it their permanent abode, at the earliest 'moment practicable. But they intended to vote. 'The Missourians were, many of them, Douglas 'men. There were 150 voters from this county, '175 from Howard, 100 from Cooper. Indeed, 'every county furnished its quota; and when 'they set out, it looked like an army. * * 'They were armed. * * * And, as there 'were no houses in the Territory, they carried 'tents. Their mission was a peaceable one—to 'vote, and to drive down stakes for their future 'homes. After the election, some 1,500 of the 'voters sent a committee to Mr. Reeder, to ascer- 'tain if it was his purpose to ratify the election. 'He answered that it was, and said the majority 'at an election must carry the day. But it is 'not to be denied that the 1,500, apprehending 'that the Governor might attempt to play the 'tyrant—since his conduct had already been in- 'sidious and unjust—wore on their hats bunches 'of hemp. They were resolved, if a tyrant at- 'tempted to trample upon the rights of the sov- 'ereign people, to hang him."

On the 29th of May, 1855, the *Squatter Sovereign*, an organ of the invasion in Missouri, thus gave utterance to its spirit:

"From reports now received of Reeder, he 'never intends returning to our borders. 'Should he do so, we, without hesitation, say 'that our people ought to hang him by the neck, 'like a traitorous dog as he is, so soon as he puts 'his unhallowed feet upon our shores.

"Vindicate your characters and the Territory; 'and should the ungrateful dog dare to come 'among us again, hang him to the first rotten 'tree.

"A military force to protect the ballot-box! 'Let President Pierce, or Governor Reeder, or 'any other power, attempt such a course in this, 'or any portion of the Union, and that day will 'never be forgotten."'

Governor Reeder, at Easton, in Pennsylvania, on his first return to that place after the elections, declared the same result in frank and candid words, which cost him his office, namely:

"It was indeed too true that Kansas had been 'invaded, conquered, subjugated, by an armed 'force from beyond her borders, led on by a fa- 'natical spirit, trampling under foot the princi- 'ples of the Kansas bill and the right of suffrage."

The Honorable David R. Atchison, a direct and out-spoken man, who never shrinks from responsibility, and who is confessedly eminent at once as a political leader in Missouri and as a leader of the Pro-Slavery movement therein directed against Kansas, in a speech reported as having been made to his fellow-citizens, and which, so far as I know, has not been disavowed, said:

"I saw it with my own eyes. These men 'came with the avowed purpose of driving or 'expelling you from the Territory. What did I 'advise you to do? Why, meet them at their 'own game. When the first election came off, I 'told you to go over and vote. You did so, and 'beat them. We, our party in Kansas, nominated 'General Whitfield. They, the Abolitionists, 'nominated Flenniken; not Flanegan, for Flan-

'egan was a good, honest man, but *Flenniken*. Well, the next day after the election, that 'that same Flenniken, with three hundred of his 'voters, left the Territory, and has never returned—no, never returned!

"Well, what next? Why, an election for 'members of the Legislature, to organize the 'Territory, must be held. What did I advise 'you to do then? Why, meet them on their 'own ground, and beat them at their own game 'again; and, cold and inclement as the weather 'was, I went over with a company of men. My 'object in going was not to vote; I had not a 'right to vote, unless I had disfranchised myself 'in Missouri. I was not within two miles of a 'voting place. My object in going was not to 'vote, but to settle a difficulty between two of 'our candidates; and Abolitionists of the North 'said, and published it abroad, that Atchison was 'there with bowie-knife and revolver, and by God ''twas true. I never did go into that Territory, I 'never intend to go into that Territory, without 'being prepared for all such kind of cattle. Well, 'we beat them; and Gov. Reeder gave certificates to a majority of all the members of both 'Houses; and then, after they were organized, as 'everybody will admit, they were the only competent persons to say who were and who were 'not members of the same."

A tree is known by its fruits. If Missourians voted in Kansas, it would be expected that the ballots deposited would exceed the number of electors. Just so it was. We have seen that it was so asserted. The Executive Journal, recently obtained, proves that in four districts, where the results were not contested, 2,964 votes were cast on the 30th of March, although only 1,365 voters were there, as ascertained by the census. Again: The Legislature chosen on the 30th of March, 1855, withdrew from the interior of the Territory to a place inconvenient to its citizens, and on the border of Missouri. There that Legislature enacted laws to this effect, namely: forbidding the speaking, writing, or printing, or publishing, of anything, in any form, calculated to disaffect slaves, or induce them to escape, under pain of not less than five years imprisonment with hard labor; and forbidding free persons from maintaining, by speech, writing, or printing, or publishing, that slaves cannot lawfully be held in the Territory, under pain of imprisonment and hard labor two years.

The Legislature further enacted, that no person "conscientiously opposed to holding slaves," or entertaining doubts of the legal existence of Slavery in Kansas, shall sit as a juror in the trial of any cause founded on a breach of the laws which I have described. They further provided, that all officers and attorneys should be sworn, not only to support the Constitution of the United States, but also to support and sustain the *organic law of the Territory*, and the *Fugitive Slave Law;* and that any persons offering to vote shall be *presumed* to be entitled to vote until the contrary is shown; and if any one, when required, shall refuse to take an oath to sustain the Fugitive Slave Law, he shall not be permitted to vote. Although they passed a law that none but an inhabitant who had paid a tax should vote, yet they made no *time* of *residence* necessary, and provided for the immediate payment of a poll tax; so virtually declaring that on the eve of an election the people of a neighboring State can come in, in unlimited numbers, and, by taking up a residence of a day or an hour, pay a poll tax, and thus become legal voters, and then, after voting, return to their own State. They thus, in practical effect, provided for the people of Missouri to control future elections at their pleasure, and permitted such only of the real inhabitants of the Territory to vote as are friendly to the holding of slaves.

They permitted no election of any of the officers in the Territory to be made by the people thereof, but created the offices, and filled them, or appointed officers to fill them, for long periods. They provided that the next annual election should be held in October, 1856, and the Assembly should meet in January, 1857; so that none of these laws could be changed until the lower House might be changed, in 1856; but the Council, which is elected for two years, could not be changed so as to allow a change of the laws or officers until the session of 1858, however much the inhabitants of the Territory might desire it. How forcibly do these laws illustrate that old political maxim of the English nation, that a Parliament called by a conqueror is itself conquered and enslaved! Who but foreigners, usurpers, and tyrants, could have made for the people of Kansas—a people "perfectly free"—such laws as these. Anatomists will describe the instrument, and even the force of the blow, if only you show them the wound.

Behold the proofs on which the allegations of invasion, usurpation, and tyranny, made by the new State of Kansas, rest. They are, first: the President's own virtual admission, by defences indirect, irrelevant, ill-tempered, sophistical, and evasive; second: an absolute agreement, concurrence, and harmony, between the statements of the conflicting parties who were engaged in the transactions involved; third: the consequences of those transactions exactly such as must follow, if the accusations be true, and such as could not result if they be false. A few words, however, must be added, to bring more distinctly into view the President's complicity in these transactions, and to establish his responsibility therefor. The President openly lent his official influence and patronage to the slaveholders of Missouri, to effect the abrogation of the prohibition of Slavery in Kansas, contained in the act of Congress of 1820. He knew their purposes in regard to the elections in Kansas. He never interfered to prevent, to defeat, or to hinder them. He employed his official patronage to aid them. He now defends and protects the usurpation and tyranny, established by the invaders in Kansas, with all the influence of his exalted station, and even with the military power of the Republic; and he argues the duty of the people there to submit to the forcible establishment of Slavery, in violation of the national pledge, which he concurred in giving, that they should be left perfectly free to reject and exclude that justly obnoxious system. It thus appears that the President of the United States holds the people of Kansas prostrate and enslaved at his feet.

To complete the painful account of this great crime, it is necessary now to add that there has not been one day nor night, since the Government of Kansas was constituted and confided to the President of the United States, in which either the properties, or the liberties, or even the lives, of its citizens have been secure against the violence and vengeance of the extreme foreign faction which he upholds and protects. At this day, Kansas is becoming, more distinctly than before, the scene of a conflict of irreconcilable opinions, to be determined by brute force. No immigrant goes there unarmed, no citizen dwells there in safety unarmed; armed masses of men are proceeding into the Territory, from various parts of the United States, to complete the work of invasion and tyranny which he has thus begun, under circumstances of fraud and perfidy unworthy of the character of a ruler of a free people. This gathering conflict in Kansas divides the sympathies, interests, passions, and prejudices, of the people of the United States. Whether, under such circumstances, it can be circumscribed within the limits of the Territory of Kansas, must be determined by statesmen from their knowledge of the courses of civil commotions, which have involved questions of moral right and conscientious duty, as well as balances of political power. Whether, on the other hand, the people of Kansas, under these circumstances, will submit to this tyranny of a citizen of the United States like themselves, whose term of political power is nearly expired, can be determined by considering it in the aspect in which it is viewed by themselves. Speechless here, as they yet are, I give utterance to their united voices, and, holding in my hand the arraignment of George III, by the Congress of 1776, I impeach—in the words of that immortal text—the President of the United States:

"He has refused to pass laws for the accommodation of the people, unless they would relinquish the right of representation in their Legislature, a right inestimable to them, and formidable to tyrants only:

"He has called together legislative bodies at a place unusual, uncomfortable, and distant from the depository of their public records, for the sole purpose of fatiguing them into compliance with his measures:

He has prevented Legislative Houses from being elected, for no other cause than his conviction that they would "oppose with manly firmness his invasions on the rights of the people:

"He has refused for a long time after" spurious Legislative Houses were imposed by himself, by usurpation, on the people of Kansas "to cause others to be elected, whereby the legislative powers, incapable of annihilation, have returned to the people at large, for their exercise, the State remaining in the mean time exposed to all the danger of invasion from without, and civil war within:

"He has created a multitude of new offices, and sent hither swarms of officers, to harass our people, and eat out their substance:

"He has kept among us, in times of peace, standing armies, to compel our submission to a foreign" Legislature, "and has affected to render the military independent of, and superior to, the civil power:

"He has combined with others to subject us to a jurisdiction foreign to our Constitution, and unacknowledged by our laws, giving his assent to their acts of pretended legislation:

"For protecting" invaders of Kansas "from punishment for any murders which they shall commit on the inhabitants" of this Territory:

"For abolishing the free system of American law in" this Territory, "establishing therein an arbitrary Government, so as to render it at once an example and fit instrument for introducing the same absolute rule into" other Territories:

"For taking away our charter, abolishing our most valuable laws, and altering fundamentally the powers of our Government:

"For suspending our own Legislature, and declaring" an usurping Legislature, constituted by himself, "invested with power to legislate for us in all cases whatsoever."

What is wanting here to fill up the complement of a high judicial process? Is it an accuser? The youngest born of the Republic is before you, imploring you to rescue her from immolation on the altar of public faction. Is it a crime? Bethink yourselves what it is that has been subverted. It is the whole of a complete and rounded-off Republican Government of a Territory indeed, by name, but, in substance, a Civil State. Consider the effect. The People of Kansas *were* "perfectly free." They now *are* free only to submit and obey. Consider whose system that Republican Government was, and the Power that established it. It was one of the Constitutions of the United States, established by an act of the Congress of the United States. Consider what a tyranny it is that has been built on that atrocious usurpation. It is not a discriminating tyranny, that selects and punishes one, or a few, or even many, but it disfranchises all, and reduces every citizen to abject slavery. Examine the code created by the Legislature. All the statutes of the State of Missouri are enacted in gross, without alteration or amendment, for the government of Kansas; and then, at the end, the hasty blunder of misnomer is corrected by an explanatory act, that wherever the word "State" occurs, it means "Territory." And what a code! One that stifles not, indeed, the fruits of the womb, but the equally important element of a State, the fruits—the immortal fruits—of the mind; a code that puts in peril all rights and liberties whatsoever, by denying to men the right to know, to utter, and to argue, freely, according to conscience—a right in itself conservative of all other rights and liberties. Is an offender wanting? He stands before you, in many respects the most eminent man in all the world—the President of the United States—the constitutional and chosen defender and protector of the people who have been subjugated and enslaved. Is there anything of dignity or authority wanting to this tribunal? Where elsewhere shall be found one more august than the Senate of the United States? It is the ancient, constant, and undoubted right and usage of Parliaments—it is the chief purpose of their being—to question and complain of all persons, of what degree soever, found grievous to the Commonwealth, in abusing the power and trust committed to them by the People. Does this tribunal need a motive? We have that, too, in painful reality. These usurpations and oppressions have hitherto rested with the President of the United States, and those whom he has abetted. If they shall be left unredressed, they will henceforth become, by adoption, our own.

The conviction of the offending President is complete, and now he sinks out of view. His punishment rests with the People of the United States, whose trust he has betrayed. His conviction was only incidental to the business which is the order of the day. The order of the day is the redress of the wrongs of Kansas.

How like unto each other are the parallels of tyranny and revolution in all countries and in all times! Kansas is to-day in the very act of revolution against a tyranny of the President of the United States, identical in all its prominent features with that tyranny of the King of England which gave birth to the American Revolution. Kansas has instituted a revolution, simply because ordinary remedies can never be applied in great political emergencies. There is a profound philosophy that belongs to revolutions. According to that philosophy, the President is assumed by the people of Kansas to entertain a resentment which can never be appeased, and his power, consequently, must be wholly taken away. Happily, however, for Kansas, and for us, her revolution is one that was anticipated and sanctioned and provided for in the Constitution of the United States, and is therefore a peaceful and (paradoxical as the expression may seem) a constitutional one. Never before have I seen occasion so great for admiring the wisdom and forecast of those who raised that noble edifice of civil government. The people of Kansas, deprived of their sovereignty by a domestic tyranny, have nevertheless lawfully rescued it provisionally, and, so exercising it, have constituted themselves a State, and applied to Congress to admit them as such into the Federal Union. Congress has power to admit the new State thus organized. The favorable exercise of that power will terminate and crown the revolution. Once a State, the people of Kansas can preserve internal order, and defend themselves against invasion. Thus, the constitutional remedy is as effectual as it is peaceful and simple.

This is the remedy for the evils existing in the Territory of Kansas, which I propose. Happily, there is no need to prove it to be either a lawful one or a proper one, or the only possible one. The President of the United States and the Committee on Territories unanimously concede all this broad ground, because he recommends it, and they adopt it.

Wherein, then, do I differ from them? Simply thus. I propose to apply the remedy now, by admitting the new State with its present population and present Constitution. My opponents insist on postponing the measure until the Territory shall be conceded by the usurping authorities to contain 93,700 inhabitants, and until those authorities shall direct and authorize the people to organize a new State, under a new Constitution. In other words, I propose to allow the people of Kansas to apply the constitutional remedy at once. The President proposes to defer it indefinitely, and to commit the entire application of it to the hands of the Missouri borderers. He confesses the inadequacy of that course by asking appropriations of money to enable him to maintain and preserve order within the Territory until the indefinite period when the constitutional remedy shall be applied. There is no sufficient reason for the delay which the President advises. He admits the rightfulness and necessity of the remedy. It is as rightful and necessary now as it ever will be. It is demanded by the condition and circumstances of the people of Kansas now. You cannot justly postpone, any more than you can justly deny, that right. To postpone would be a denial. The President will need no grant of money, or of armed men, to enforce obedience to law, when you shall have redressed the wrongs of which the People complain. Even under Governments less free than our own, there is no need of power where justice holds the helm. When justice is impartially administered, the obedience of the subject or citizen will be voluntary, cheerful, and practically unlimited. Freedom justly due cannot be conceded too soon. True freedom exists, the utmost bounds of civil liberty are obtained, only where complaints are freely heard, deeply considered, and speedily redressed. So only can you restore to Kansas the perfect freedom which you pledged, and she has lost.

The Constitution does not prescribe 93,700, or any other number of people, as necessary to constitute a State. Besides, under the present ratio of increase, Kansas, whose population now is 40,000, will number 100,000 in a few months. The point made concerning numbers is therefore practically unimportant and frivolous. The President objects that the past proceedings, by which the new state of Kansas was organized, were irregular in three respects: First. That they were instituted, conducted, and completed, without a previous permission by Congress, or by the local authorities within the Territory. Secondly. That they were instituted, conducted, and completed, by a party, and not by the whole people of Kansas; and, thirdly, that the new State holds an attitude of defiance and insubordination towards the Territorial authorities and the Federal Union. I reply, first, that if the proceedings in question were irregular and partisanlike and factious, the exigencies of the case would at least excuse the faults, and Congress has unlimited discretion to waive them. Secondly. The proceedings were not thus irregular, partisanlike, and factious, because no act of Congress forbade them—no act of the Territorial Legislature forbade them, directly or by implication—nor had the Territorial Legislature power either to authorize or to prohibit them. The proceedings were, indeed, instituted by a party who favored them. But they were prosecuted and consummated in the customary forms of popular elections, which were open to all the inhabitants of the Territory qualified to vote by the organic law, and to no others; and they have in no case come into conflict, nor does the new State now act or assume to engage in conflict with either the Territorial authorities or the Government of the Union. Thirdly. There can be no irregularity where there is no law prescribing what shall be regular. Congress has passed no law establishing regulations for the organization or admission of new States. Precedents in such cases, being without foundation in law, are without authority. This is a country whose Government is regulated, not by precedents, but by Constitutions. But if precedents were necessary, they are found in the cases of Texas and California, each of which was organized and admitted, subject to the same alleged irregularities.

The majority of the Committee on Territories, in behalf of the President, interpose one further objection, by tracing this new State organization to the influence of a secret, armed, political society. Secrecy and combination, with extra-judicial oaths and armed power, were the enginery of the Missouri borderers in effecting the subjugation of the people of Kansas, as that machinery is always employed in the commission of political crimes. How far it was lawful or morally right for the people of Kansas to employ the same agencies for the defence of their lives and liberties, may be a question for casuists, but certainly is not one for me. I can freely confess, however, my deep regret that secret societies for any purpose whatsoever have obtained a place among political organizations within the Republic; and it is my hope that the experience which we have now so distinctly had, that they can be but too easily adapted to unlawful, seditious, and dangerous enterprises, while they bring down suspicion and censure on high and noble causes when identified with them, may be sufficient to induce a general discontinuance of them.

Will the Senate hesitate for an hour between the alternatives before them? The passions of the American People find healthful exercise in peaceful colonizations, and the construction of railroads, and the building up and multiplying of republican institutions. The Territory of Kansas lies across the path through which railroads must be built, and along which such institutions must be founded, without delay, in order to preserve the integrity of our Empire. Shall we suppress enterprises so benevolent and so healthful, and inflame our country with that fever of intestine war which exhausts and consumes not more the wealth and strength than the virtue and freedom of a nation? Shall we confess that the proclamation of popular sovereignty within the Territory of Kansas was not merely a failure, but was a pretence and a fraud? Or will Senators now contend that the people of Kansas, destitute as they are of a Legislature of their own, of Executive authorities of their own, of Judicial authorities of their own, of a militia of their own, of revenues of their own subject to disposal by themselves, practically deprived as they are of the rights of voting, serving as jurors, and of writing, printing, and speaking, their own opinions, are nevertheless in the enjoyment and exercise of popular sovereignty? Shall we confess before the world, after so brief a trial, that this great political system of ours is inadequate either to enable the majority to control through the operation of opinion, without force, or to give security to the citizen against tyranny and domestic violence? Are we prepared so soon to relinquish our simple and beautiful systems of republican government, and to substitute in their place the machinery of usurpation and despotism?

The Congress of the United States can refuse admission to Kansas only on the ground that it will not relinquish the hope of carrying African Slavery into that new Territory. If you are prepared to assume that ground, why not do it manfully and consistently, and establish Slavery there by a direct and explicit act of Congress? But have we come to that stage of demoralization and degeneracy so soon? We, who commenced our political existence and gained the sympathies of the world by proclaiming to other nations that we held "these truths to be self-evident: That 'all men are born equal, and have certain inalien-'able rights; and that among these rights are 'life, liberty, and the pursuit of happiness:" we, who in the spirit of that declaration have assumed to teach and to illustrate, for the benefit of mankind, a higher and better civilization than they have hitherto known! If the Congress of the United States shall persist in this attempt, then they shall at least allow me to predict its results. Either you will not establish African Slavery in Kansas, or you will do it at the cost of the sacrifice of all the existing liberties of the American people. Even if Slavery were, what it is not, a boon to the people of Kansas, they would reject it if enforced upon their acceptance by Federal bayonets. The attempt is in conflict with all the tendencies of the age. African Slavery has, for the last fifty years, been giving way, as well in this country as in the islands and on the main land throughout this hemisphere. The political power and prestige of Slavery in the United States are passing away. The slave States practically governed the Union directly for fifty years. They govern it now, only indirectly, through the agency of Northern hands, temporarily enlisted in their support. So much, owing to the decline of their power, they have already conceded to the free States. The next step, if they persist in their present course, will be the resumption and exercise by the free States of the control of the Government, without such concessions as they have hitherto made to obtain it. Throughout a period of nearly twenty years, the defenders of Slavery screened it from discussion in the national councils. Now, they practically confess to the necessity for defending it here, by initiating discussion themselves. They have at once thrown away their most successful weapon, compromise, and worn out that one which was next in effectiveness, threats of secession from the Union. It is under such unpropitious circumstances that they begin the new experiment of extending Slavery into free territory by force, the armed power of the Federal Government. You will need many votes from free States in the House of Representatives, and even some votes from those States in this House, to send an army with a retinue of slaves in its train into Kansas. Have you counted up your votes in the two Houses? Have you calculated how long those who shall cast such votes will retain their places in the National Legislature?

But I will grant, for the sake of the argument, that with Federal battalions you can carry Slavery into Kansas, and maintain it there. Are you quite confident that this republican form of government can then be upheld and preserved? You will then yourselves have introduced the Trojan horse. No republican Government ever has endured, with standing armies maintained in its bosom to enforce submission to its laws. A people who have once learned to relinquish their rights, under compulsion, will not be long in forgetting that they ever had any. In extending Slavery into Kansas, therefore, by arms, you will subvert the liberties of the people.

Senators of the free States, I appeal to you. Believe ye the prophets? I know you do. You know, then, that Slavery neither works mines and quarries, nor founds cities, nor builds ships, nor levies armies, nor mans navies. Why, then, will you insist on closing up this new Territory of Kansas against all enriching streams of immigration, while you pour into it the turbid and poisonous waters of African Slavery? Which one of you all, whether of Connecticut, or of Pennsylvania, or of Illinois, or of Michigan, would consent thus to extinguish the chief light of civilization within the State in which your own fortunes are cast, and in which your own posterity are to live? Why will you pursue a policy so unkind, so ungenerous, and so unjust, towards the helpless, defenceless, struggling Territory of Kansas, inhabited as it is by your own brethren, depending on you for protection and safety? Will Slavery in Kansas add to the wealth or power of your own States, or to the wealth, power, or glory, of the Republic? You know that it will diminish all of these. You profess a desire to end this national debate about Slavery, which has become, for you, intolerable. Is it not time to relinquish that hope? You have exhausted the virtue, for that purpose, that resided in compacts and platforms, in the suppression of the right of petition and in arbitrary parliamentary laws, and in abnegation of Federal authority over the subject of Slavery within the National Territories. Will you even then end the debate, by binding Kansas with chains, for the safety of Slavery in Missouri? Even then you must give over Utah to Slavery, to make it secure and permanent in Kansas; and you must give over Oregon and Washington to both Polygamy and Slavery, so as to guaranty equally the one and the other of those peculiar domestic institutions in Utah; and so you must go on, sacrificing on the shrine of peace Territory after Territory, until the prevailing nationality of freedom and of virtue shall be lost, and the vicious anomalies, which you have hitherto vainly hoped Almighty Wisdom would remove from among you without your own concurrence, shall become the controlling elements in the Republic. He who found a river in his path, and sat down to wait for the flood to pass away, was not more unwise than he who expects the agitation of Slavery to cease, while the love of Freedom animates the bosoms of mankind.

The solemnity of the occasion draws over our heads that cloud of disunion, which always arises whenever the subject of Slavery is agitated. Still, the debate goes on, more ardently, earnestly, and angrily, than ever before. It employs now not merely logic, reproach, menace, retort, and defiance, but sabres, rifles, and cannon. Do you look through this incipient war quite to the end, and see there peace, quiet, and harmony, on the subject of Slavery? If so, pray enlighten me, and show me how long the way is which leads to that repose. The free States are loyal, and they always will remain so. Their foothold on this Continent is firm and sure. Their ability to maintain themselves, unaided, under the present Constitution, is established. The slave States, also, have been loyal hitherto, and I hope and trust they ever may remain so. But if disunion could ever come, it would come in the form of a secession of the slaveholding States; and it would come, then, when the slaveholding power, which is already firmly established on the Gulf of Mexico, and extends a thousand miles northward along both banks of the Mississippi, should have fastened its grappling irons upon the fountains of the Missouri and the slopes of the Rocky Mountains. Then that power would either be intolerably supreme in this Republic, or it would strike for independence or exclusive domination. Then the free States and slave States of the Atlantic, divided and warring with each other, would disgust the free States of the Pacific, and they would have abundant cause and justification for withdrawing from a Union productive no longer of peace, safety, and liberty to themselves, and no longer holding up the cherished hopes of mankind.

Mr. President, the Continental Congress of 1787, on resigning the trust, which it had discharged with signal fidelity, into the hands of the authorities elected under the new Constitution, and in taking leave of their constituents, addressed to the people of the United States this memorable injunction: "Let it never be forgot-'ten, that the cause of the United States has 'always been the cause of human nature." Let us recall that precious monition; let us examine the ways which we have pursued hitherto, under the light thrown upon them by that instruction. We shall find, in doing so, that we have forgotten moral right, in the pursuit of material greatness, and we shall cease henceforth from practicing upon ourselves the miserable delusion, that we can safely extend Empire, when we shall have become reckless of the obligations of Eternal Justice, and faithless to the interests of Universal Freedom.

TO THE OPPONENTS OF SLAVERY-EXTENSION.

The Publishing Association of Washington intend to stereotype the Speeches delivered in Congress during the present session, and other Documents, suitable for use in the coming Presidential Campaign. In order to facilitate their circulation as much as possible, the Association will furnish and mail them, singly, to such names and post offices as may be desired, at one dollar per hundred for documents of eight pages, and two dollars per hundred for documents of sixteen pages, free of postage. For packages of one hundred, or more, sent at the cost of purchasers, documents of eight pages, sixty-two cents, and documents of sixteen pages, one dollar and twenty-five cents.

Persons sending us ten dollars and upwards can have the amount placed to their credit, and copies of each Speech or Document issued by the Association during the Campaign will be sent to their address or to such names as they may direct, in such quantities as may be desired, until the money sent is exhausted. Address

LEWIS CLEPHANE, *Secretary*,
Washington, D. C

BUELL & BLANCHARD, Printers, Washington, D. C.

www.ingramcontent.com/pod-product-compliance
Lightning Source LLC
LaVergne TN
LVHW020643110826
845149LV00004B/1343
* 9 7 8 1 4 1 8 1 8 9 9 6 9 *